Believing is not the same as Being Saved

Believing is not the same as Being Saved

LISA MARTIN

 The University of Alberta Press

Published by

The University of Alberta Press
Ring House 2
Edmonton, Alberta, Canada T6G 2E1
www.uap.ualberta.ca

LIBRARY AND ARCHIVES CANADA CATALOGUING IN PUBLICATION

Martin, Lisa, 1979-, author
     Believing is not the same as being saved / Lisa Martin.

(Robert Kroetsch series)
Issued in print and electronic formats.
ISBN 978-1-77212-187-2 (softcover).—
ISBN 978-1-77212-315-9 (PDF).—
ISBN 978-1-77212-329-6 (EPUB).—
ISBN 978-1-77212-330-2 (Kindle)
     I. Title. II. Series: Robert Kroetsch series

PS8626.A77247B45 2017   C811'.6   C2016-907891-4
                                             C2016-907892-2

First edition, first printing, 2017.

First printed and bound in Canada by Houghton Boston Printers, Saskatoon, Saskatchewan.
Copyediting and proofreading by Peter Midgley.
A volume in the Robert Kroetsch Series.

The University of Alberta Press gratefully acknowledges the support received for its publishing program from the Government of Canada, the Canada Council for the Arts, and the Government of Alberta through the Alberta Media Fund.

Canada Canada Council Conseil des Arts for the Arts du Canada   Alberta Government

from "The Brothers Get Acquainted"

"Half your work is done and acquired, Ivan: you love life.
Now you need only apply yourself to the second half, and you are saved."

"You're already saving me, though maybe I wasn't perishing. And what does
this second half consist of?"

"Resurrecting your dead, who may never have died."

FYODOR DOSTOEVSKY

The Brothers Karamazov (1880), trans. Pevear and Volokhonsky, 1990

Contents

Believing is not the same as being saved

The summer I was fifteen a girl at my church camp
fell from the high rock where she'd been lying
in the sun. I heard the news on the phone
which rang in a room where I was trying to die
without technically killing myself: it was an age
at which much of what we did passed as pleasure
but was actually terror. The girl who fell punctured
the room with a question: *is this really what you
want?* Her scream loud enough to travel
an hour's hike away to where the tanned, shirtless
boys' counsellor dressing by the fire recognized
its message. He ran the entire distance in bare feet,
a pair of worn shorts, sweat rising to the surface.
He was a teenager himself—each footfall

bearing him toward the absolute far edge of youth,
strength. He gathered her in his arms, carried her
body to camp, despite everything. He ran, even then,
though what compelled him had altered, though his
muscles changed, became the animal necessity
we need to get through. Her death cradled to him
like the child of his own he would one day hold, and no
doubt, love. The news came, in the room where I sat,
and then went. And did I gain courage? I knew
the exact quality of light on the surface of that rock.
Each night at camp, the year before, I'd walked
silent amidst the roving beams of flashlights
on the same trail of mulch, moss, rock, not knowing
the choice I would one day run toward, then—

irrevocably, turn from. After that, I absorbed
air, knowledge, like dew—testing God against
all better judgement. I started thinking that summer
of cedar bark and stones, the texture of the path
beneath the feet of the boys' counsellor as he
ran—I believe he felt everything—carrying her
death and love with his body as only the
living can. I flicked off a switch that summer
as I walked. I wanted to understand
darkness, the quality of my heart: not light,
but spark. Even then, the path I was on
extended far past the limit suggested
by the way the path curved gently toward
the bright fire, voices singing softly

in darkness not inflected yet with the cry
of her voice falling impossible through air that
couldn't catch her. Even now, what I want most
isn't to walk past that song into knowledge.
Believe me: I want to sing, despite
everything. I want to believe
we all could be saved.

I

One hundred ways to build
the world

Even these decades later, when I think of my first day
at school, I think of two boys who claimed to know
something I didn't: the highest number. *Infinity*, said
the first boy, dismissing me, my world of real numbers.
Later, in a church service in my parents' basement, sitting
in a row of chairs with the others, facing the wood-burning
stove, I intuited the secret: how to advance, case by case,
from *20* to *30* to *40*, by way of adding only what I already
knew. *Infinity plus one*, said the other boy, outdoing the first.
And I felt my certainty vanish. In the basement I saw the crisis
before I touched its cusp. Approaching the far side of *99*,
I sensed its possibility. And, though I didn't know—

this would one day be true—I can still see the grey
smudged moons my eraser shed on paper that first day
at school. Effacing the numbers I knew, not seeing
they were themselves answers. Sparks in the woodstove
popped hard and orange against that glass, then fell, ash
soft. *One hundred*, I said, aloud, the grown-ups around me
probably praying. I only added the numbers *1* through *9*
to the highest numbers I knew, then did it again—
but found I could build the world that way,
out of what I had.

One thing

It all happened here: enough to brand
the heart. All the first things. Southeast
of Saskatoon, past ball diamonds of hammered
dust, and fields the after-winter hue
of a green too fatigued to promise spring
in that place I can only now lay claim to,
that only love can now lay claim to, it had
always been enough to save one thing.

All winter, in the cellar with earth walls,
my parents kept the musk of decaying soil
in red plastic buckets that lined the cellar walls.
It had always been enough to last the long winter.
In spring, the wheelbarrow stood in the garden
holding the least three-eyed potatoes of winter,
dirt and meagreness, winter-blind: my parents
cut them up with a spade,

planted them eye-side-up in the dust.
Dead leaves and seed pods scuttled down
the sidewalk, letting go the need to survive:
a lesson we wouldn't learn for some time.
Even the exhausted soil kept giving
the little that it had away. We held on
to the one thing: I'm not sure
we called it that, at the time.

Firsts and lasts

The last summer of my childhood I didn't know what to look for, wasn't told I should spend the days collecting things I might never see again. So I can still see the way the dust in our unplanted garden looked when it first began to rain, but I've forgotten what Dad's voice sounded like when he said my name. When I think of that summer, I think of long days spent alone in the yard, in the midst of a longer illness. How my knees took on the imprint of ants, the long grass. That July was the first time I noticed heat, how it holds you by the neck, the back of the knees, and won't let go. Hot even at night. Cool air a swarm of bees crowding dazed around you. In the day, a sunburn, a piece of ice to suck. Hum of decayed blooms, of what is left when beauty fails. Bloodstained shirts. A dark room with a fan, and on the table, a Tupperware bowl kept within reach. All summer, Mom rinsed that bowl, which smelled of bile. Dad was up all night, so she was too. For the first and last time, they let us stay by ourselves outside in the camper, so we could sleep. We sat at the fold-out table and ate heat-curled carrot sticks, drank watery fruit juice, cracking the slivers of ice in our teeth. On a night so hot I got up three times for more ice, Mom took me into the backyard. *Look,* she said. I'd never seen so many stars. She held me to her side, her palm cool on my skin, pointed to the star-covered sky, a map. *Is there anything up there you recognize?* She showed me the Big Dipper, the sky's bright ladle, and its sister, the Little Dipper. She told me they would be there anytime I looked, those cool bright stars, portioning out a share of light. And then she squeezed my shoulders, drew me back toward the house. As if it were up to me, after this, to find my own way. That was her tone—one quick lesson, then it's up to you.

Even now, when I see the Big Dipper, it's often a surprise. On a clear night, I think of her, of the summer that stretched into the winter he died, and the summers beyond that. Sometimes the Dipper's upside down, sometimes it's not. And I try to remember, but I can't, the way it looked that first night. The kind of thing a child doesn't think to notice, which way the signs are pointing.

Pool

The week after the funeral
a swimming pool green as
my father's eyes. We dove
in pulled our small selves
through the chlorinated
depths our submerged bodies
releasing joy involuntary
underwater wriggling free
of gravity. Each evening
our mother combed wet
tangled hair applied Band Aids
to cuts in feet the pool floor
stuccoed our joy not protecting us
from damage we did not feel
as we incurred it yet suffered for
later dry and tucked in kissed
goodnight. My father's eyes
weren't green but brown it hurt
at the time we just kept
swimming each morning
we woke eager, hurt more
than the night before.

Map for the road home

A tractor ploughs up dust in an empty field.
The last of the light has gone down. We drive past,
cross the river late—thinking nothing, not the structure
of the bridge will hold us, not what kind of a thing
is trust—just remembering sun over wetlands,
the land itself long and low, and leaning
beneath sky. Last light like oil in an old lamp
smudges the sky on its way out—smoky pink,
ochre, grey. And the first thing you say,
out of silence—is the Dutch phrase for *sorry*.
The words mean *it grieves me*, and we go back
to watching the ruts of the road feed themselves
beneath tires, which are ceaselessly grinding
snow and salt. Shapes appear at the side
of the road, waiting to run out, get hit—
shapes that vanish on the approach.

Remind me: is this how it always goes?
There's a way of speaking as if the difference
matters, as if the road home is finite—everything
begins and ends somewhere, like your hand
in mine, or how last light fractures in the limbs
of pine—while beyond my window, a coyote
follows a trail into the dusk that only it can see.
Its path marks the place where the mind gives up
on what it knows. There are words for this
in many different languages. *Het spijt me*,
you say, *I'm sorry*, or *it grieves me*, or *what
difference does it make?* The coyote yelps, looking
for the place where things die out. The mind
seeks a place where it can learn to lie down.

Memorial at Horseshoe Lake

This morning, when on the far side
of a frozen lake we found five candles
flickering in wind, pools of red wax
with seconds left of flame, I asked you
how long you thought it could last
and you said nothing. So we watched
as the small fires downed their sparks,
hissing slightly, bending charred wicks
to touch the cooling surface of wax—
one by one, extinguishing themselves.
I thought someone might come back.
Someone who—having walked no farther
than a distance traversable in the time it takes
for five candles marking a lost place
to burn down their lengths—might return,
wanting proof, or to stare at the improbable
flame, excruciating hope, wanting
to watch it burn. Beside a frozen lake,
a memorial anonymous as wind, blowing
in the grooves of being left alone and
the marks it makes in snow.

The Ascension

I was given object lessons. Shown how oil and water will not mix.
This was to teach the separation from the body. Slick of motor oil, the water's stained

skin. I tried it for myself: shook and shook, so hard I developed stigmata—
cracks in my palms where the skin became a desert, cracked clay.

Christ walked on water to prove faith too is about density.
About what can be held within the body. Knowledge is heavy.

So the balance can be tipped in anyone's favour, like salt in a glass
settling toward the bottom. Substances that are more dense will sink beneath those

that are less. Oil always makes its way to the surface of the water.
A barge, though heavy, floats in the dull grey harbour.

Yesterday I found a grebe drenched in oil, skim of sand and foam. Dead on the shore.
Faith and doubt—like evaporation, condensation. Each occurs at the other's

threshold. Christ, at the end of his life, was heavier than he'd ever been.
He hung from his hands until he died, denser than air. How much

difficult knowledge can a body hold? Because substances that are more dense
sink beneath those that are less. After the crucifixion, Christ rises again.

This is his destiny. Ascending above the multitude, he achieves his immortality.
But then the crowd goes home. He has been changed by love.

His needs have grown too human. Alone, he reaches the upper
atmosphere, which is cold and thin. No one hears

his miracle fail him. But there is a cry, *Eloi*.
As he falls, the oil that can't be washed anoints his body.

Perspective

A Dodge on the dirt road packed with snow, ice. A child in the back of
the car wrapped in the wool blanket they have kept in the trunk for days
as cold as this. She stares out the backseat window, tries to watch one
snowflake as it falls, but it falls too fast, blurs with the others. She's heard
a rumour she'd like to disprove, finds it hard to believe anyone's checked.
It doesn't fit with the other evidence. Hills the same for miles, and the sky.
She's interested in the question of flight, wires strung high for as far as
she can see. She loves to watch them crest and fall. She's seen how they
dip and dart and sag from pole to pole, like woodpeckers. She thinks, *they
are dead trees, trees with no branches, leaves.* The child has watched them for
a long time now. She wishes she could tell how long, the only landmark
these constant fences, crows on the posts taking flight. A long time in
the future, twenty years or more, she'll board a train in a small station,
northern BC. She'll ride alone, up all night, beneath the moon, the light
of the train cutting an arc through pristine forest. Lodgepole pine, white
spruce. Snow in their limbs. Land so otherwise untouched it's like riding
through a whisper. Then: cutting through town, seeing the storm-toppled
pole, wires dragged down, wrapped loose around it like torn muscles, a
strangled beast. The blizzard thick around her and the highway nowhere
in sight. She wonders how her dad can drive through it, how he knows
where the road goes. Holds in her mind an amazement she knows she
will soon outgrow. A faith that is young, incomplete.

Sonnet for what we resolve into—

God said: Let there be light, a leak to let
out darkness. So it was that God became
the lesser creatures, predator that preyed,
fossil record, ultrasonic bounces, blue
light. So God assumed the form of a hurt
thing with legs, dragging its pain onto
shore; so certain voices can't be heard at
all, underwater. So, when it rains, all the
basements flood. And God, knee-deep in it,
wonders *Is this still me?* while I wield the
vacuum, suck the warped linoleum dry.
Somewhere, someone dies again and I think
there went another piece of me. What split
from God? Not light, but brilliance: you, me.

A solstice is an astronomical event

It's been nearly eight years since you died—
and each time the earth swings past this close
to the sun, I feel the push of exclusion, years
accumulated between us like layers on rock,
rusted red sediments, granite faults, while
earth turns away from sun. Position is not
the same as instance. Each winter's freeze/thaw
knocks certain relentless accidents loose

and I am slowly becoming someone
you have never known. Proximity reminds
that nearness alone is not intimate. Do solitary
rocks, in darkness, desire to remain as they are,
and therefore whole? Surely even rock must want
the cold that enters, cracks it open at the fault.

Story

The afghan grew knot by knot, a kind of calendar. *Four rows yellow, four pale green, four the colour of black spruce.* Long afternoons, a sofa, slant light through pine needles, blanket the colour of the seasons as they pass, prairie wind at the glass.

This is a story of the kind of failure that is most ordinary—the dream of a future worth having: then he grew sick. Enough to lie all day stretched out on that sofa. Her blanket tucked around him as carefully as it had been made. His mind drifted—so he pictured their children grown old, asked for the impossible. From the dark basement, a child dragged the heavy storm door, made of wood splintered by weather. There is a stripe in the blanket that reveals how much this hurt. The father, no longer able, a flawed row. His sickness, her afghan, the space heater drawn too close.

And so the story goes. The blanket burned: melted like a skin. She hid it, years after, in the back of the linen closet, with sheets that smelled of disuse. Later, I put it in a box with the last of her things, brought it home so I could finger the knots in the yarn, scars of the hidden burn, and think of her. Before she was a mother, she made this, the blanket stretching over her stomach as it grew.

Late in the afternoon, she hummed a half-remembered tune, while a kettle whistled in the other room. Now the afghan's on my sofa; it's in my living room.

Return

Signs of what's leaving, bruised apples in the grass, sunflowers out back
thick and stoop-shouldered, despite deep-green stalks strong as wrists.

The man, or woman, you love is leaving, dust-blue sky, the car
parked in the yard covered in a sheet, last year's leaves.

Over sparse grass, a butterfly, a flame in a cold room, flickers.
The car parked on the lawn beneath a dust-blue sheet. It gathers

seasons, chokecherries, a severed branch. Hurt dog, a thin whimper: it is time.
A season's shed skin—needle-cloak of pine, scattered birdsong, rabbit fur, leaves.

Time I paid attention. Ballparks, white chalk in the grass. What we love we know
only as it's leaving. Puddles in the pavement, the sunflowers' drooped heads—

they've given up on us, on *this time around things are gonna be
different*. Grey sidewalks wet with rain nothing ever solid nothing breaks.

Boughs as old as the house, apples the colour of a child's cold cheek.
What has turned away now goes swiftly in the other direction.

Blade of winter. A pale throat, air the colour of vanished birds.
The blush of arrival, of *it is time*. There is no going back.

What reaches forward, always longing—its demands will not be met.
Too late we recognize our ordinary hearts, the afternoon's long shadow,

a blue jay's tracks in first snow. Nostalgia's too late, comes
with arms bare wanting what's gone. Wind and dead

leaves, ash, smoke. Not even if we'd known.

River

A gutter, a place for run-off when the land is full.
A form of patience. A way of taking it when the rain won't stop.
A kind of mother. The river, when I saw it, was dragging several uprooted trees.
My mother could take hatred and make it forgiveness.
I never considered precipitates, the fallout of conversions like this.
River something you take for granted, a milky green
muscle, a mentality—strength not for the sake
of glory, but for the sake of being ready.
The kind of strength that could carry away a city
just by slowly overflowing its banks, filling up
with what surrounds it. My mother was like this, a reservoir;
she swallowed pain like a river bank in a flash flood,
swelled with it; one day, she exceeded her body.
It is important to remember that it hurt.
That a river tears itself on what it touches,
that this is what it is to be a river.

It would be easier if I could forget,
if the river, the slow gull-cry
of what will happen next—

if the sound of river, stones.

Bill of Rights

In the hallway outside her room, on foolscap,
pinned directly to the drywall, *a dying person has a right*
to a painless death. This hangs parallel to a picture on the opposite
wall, taken the year before—of the two of us. Her hair styled
in waves that frame her face, my hair covered by blue cloth, stars.
A dying person has a right to things not as they are, but as they were—
these two things like sibling stones that used to be one stone,
and still fit each other's hollows, jagged in the gap where the single
rock split apart, its edges crumbling into schist, disintegrating
according to the strongest possible physical law.

A dying person has a right for the shape she has formed in her mind
of the stone to match the shape of the stone before it was broken.
She has a right to dignity, to cover her bare head with a blue cloth—
with the one I'm wearing in the photo taken the year before that
hangs outside her room, opposite the *Dying Person's Bill of Rights.*
It looks like the ocean, she tells me, not like the night,
though the cloth is dark, blue, covered with stars.
She has a right to see things like this, to see
in the muted painfulness of the stars
her own brilliant dying. A right to
things at this distance.

Singing in the spirit

During the rain, she sits on the mat inside the screen door, listening
to the raindrops moderate. Their shifting music. She listens until she
can hear different sections of the orchestra, each by its own surfaces—
the rooftops, eavestroughs, the sewer section, the cars with their tires
uselessly grinding the water. Just when she thinks the music can't get
any louder, a low cloud empties itself onto a patch of grass behind her
neighbour's house, filling a hole where the silence had been waiting
for her, waiting to tell her something she needed to know. Now she'll
never hear it. Instead, she hears the streetlamp click on and off according
to its timed circuit, washing the road the cars and the rain in a pale
orange light. Sometimes, what is there on the other side of the screen
becomes too much for her. When this happens—it has happened before—
when the rain leaps back a foot above the pavement, demonstrating
its lack of height, how utterly fallen it has become—when the street is
converted to a small river—when the knowledge of what can be washed
away—of what can't—when the music stops and starts and the rain
continues—she puts her hands around her head the way you might hold
the head of someone you love, who is very sick. She sings to it, sings in
the spirit, the rain's music. Holds it like a gentle thing, a bird, something
she could lose, something that could be broken or lost too easily.

The song of the spirit drawing near to the body

The smell of the rain through the screen and through the dust of the screen. And after, the smell of it lingering outside near the brick of the house, in the garden with its soaked flowers. She'd been waiting for this storm to come. Waiting without knowing that this was what she was doing. Thinking she was stirring the pot of soup on the stove. With the long spoon waiting for the green halves of peas to give up their shape. But then the rain came, thunder like a jaw letting go. She ran out into the street and it slipped past her, went right up to the front door of the house. On its way, splashing her feet in their plain sandals. Getting at the places between the toes where the dust had been. After, the smell of the rain in her hair. She woke to the metal taste on her tongue, the disappointing sound of a storm that has died down. Working away at it now, the passion lost in the downpour. Waking, she was aware of dreaming of a time before she was born. Remembering at last how to enter her life. How it was done the first time. Pushing in the dark, in through the walls of the house. Coming into the room where the woman lay sweating, about to give birth. Pushing into her like a dandelion breaking through concrete. Like grass through a driveway, like grass anywhere.

A small sigh, a hard thought, enters

In the end, she is left with the rain falling in the street outside her house—the heavy, staccato fists beating the dust. She is left sitting in the dark staring at the backs of her hands, at the blue veins in her hands that have started to look so old, like her mother's. Somewhere a spirit empties itself of what it loves. The rain falls with a sound like a garbage bag with the bottom ripping out, everything splashing down. She is sitting with an emptied heart waiting to fill up with what is left. Rain making the sound things make on their way out, a sound like poverty, dysentery, like something that will hull you. The man downstairs is beating his dog. The woman was once an infant the weight of a small rock, and she has grown into this: the dog yelps, and she does nothing. The dog howls, making the sound of the dawning of knowledge that is not understood. Somewhere a boy on a beach holds a smooth green stone and wonders where it came from. The woman opens her mouth and a small sigh, a hard thought, enters. She hears the smack and howl of the man and his dog and she hears the storm. Waits until the noises stop, praying for courage. Instead she finds the place it belongs in her heart and has left her, the shape like a small hand clutching a thumb.

Individualism

The North Thompson river west
of Valemount—in the place of its birth—
is ancient as the rock that cradles it.
But it is also young, as young as this rain.
This river began as a bead of sweat formed
in the collarbone hollow of the Rockies—
as relief, warm from its birth, a praise song
of rain and moss, a pool of light that would soon
pull south, building muscle; now it ligaments
the high country—desert scrub, cactus, dry rock—
it praises the cracked ribs of the land
with the moisture of its body.

Each day it not only begins, but disappears,
leaving along the same valley as the highway.
Watching, you can feel it turn its back and walk away
like the friend you last saw at an airport departure gate
and never saw again, though a year later
she got off a different plane, and said hello;
so the river is always becoming
something else, something both familiar
and unknown: a copious leaving.
What you recognize is no part of it.
The river comes and goes;
it empties into rain,
and other rivers.

Bearings

Must be after midnight the world outside the study window's gone black.
A new moon in disguise, unopened eye. At the bottom of the screen—

night moths. Wings beige like a dead woman's shoes. They shudder
against the mesh, feel with lash-thin feet for a flaw, something insecure,

a way to enter the room. Black behind their wings makes a move
for the holes in the screen too small for moths to slip through.

The woman used to catch them fluttering at the ceiling with her hands,
coax them back into the night where they belong. Now she's gone—

no one here to flick off the light, return attention to the absent moon, shiver
of wings. One still light is all they're after, what helps them stay on course.

No one to sit with in the dark tonight, to watch the stark field of their attraction
go slack. Listen—they have stopped rustling across the screen. In the garden

the white night-blooming moonflower holds its pale-dish face to the sky.
The moths will find it, pollinate it, and move on. But what will I do?

The moonflower's silver white gleaming will not be enough.
Nor will the moon itself—when it reappears as a sliver of light

curl of a child's hair fallen on the kitchen floor. Nor will the late
summer sun, as it approaches. Nor, in winter, the bare

bulb against the house. Nor any other luminous thing.

Survival and all other possibles

To survive, we migrate: songbirds, indelible
silver-bright salmon (also known as dog, or keta,
a variety of chum), human beings, whoever we are
we leave our origin, the imprint of us, a scent
in sand; our native sense of balance tilting
with departure, leaving us nauseous with
purpose, homing. On migration, all possible
experts disagree: do we move *toward* or
away from? My four-year-old daughter returns
from preschool with her own image, the word
PROOF stamped across her face. *Yes,* I think
in the dim kitchen, but *of what?* In physics, no

force exists in isolation. Instead: vectors travel equally
in opposite directions, like ideal political parties,
heartfelt grief. So gravity co-exists with what
opposes it, the ol' Force Normal that keeps us
upright, groundless. We fight, or else, we fly—
like passerines, the orphan in Gillian Welch's
quavering vocals: What moves you? Love?
Art? Do you still believe in anything unmoved?
Is anything in you transfused or -fixed by glare
on windshield or high-rise—late pink sun
reflecting the day's end as beauty
or blindness—

anything surviving that will not die?
p.s. George Monbiot says *if you fly, you destroy other people's* [blank]. This is and is not a test. We migrate, love, even if it kills us. And yet, I still feel I might be confusing love with something else (*con-fuse, v. to mix together*) perhaps even with its opposite which is above all else the risk, isn't it, the one we take.

If we understand the laws at all

we understand this: at last, winter's receding
even if snow hasn't yet; and sun always thaws
what it can (if slowly) so each day has
another inch in it, of ground. So grief, too,
recedes, just when we have stopped believing
what leaves must always shake us. Such laws we
understand (if at all) through consequence,

effect. If a breeze arises to carry
warmth to our bodies, there must also
somewhere be bodies the breeze can't reach.
Let there be wind because of what the season's
spent. Something must drag the wound away
from itself; lift snow from grass, expose debris.

Still life with white roses

The glass vase in the centre of my table, my life, holds twelve white roses. In the window, their blurred image, glow of the lamp, our bodies moving past. I hold her and walk past the roses, her sick head curled into my neck, heat absorbed rather than reflected. The roses are only white in that most obvious sense. Some of the petals are blue like the blue veins at the bridge of the baby's nose, where the skin is so thin the blood shows through. She whimpers, tries to fall asleep, and I drink as much water as I can stand so there will be enough milk to soothe her, provide relief. The petals of the roses are healthy and fat at the centre, and she and I are lucky in this world. When her fever spikes I take a bowl that was once my mother's and fill it with water. The roses have taken only a little of what I have given them, as if they sense the coming end through their blunt stems. I wet her hair, sop her soft back, wipe the clammy bottoms of her feet. Ringing the cloth into the bowl that used to be my mother's, I prolong the ritual for the sound those drops of water make landing in the bowl, a sound as old as the blood that's too hot in her body and I'm so lost from love and lack of sleep this could be a story I'm in, such an old story I don't remember anymore how it ends.

Some of the petals are pale like the first light that burns febrile through the kitchen window as we walk toward morning. I hold her close to feed her, and these small feet could be the Lord's feet, white roses wilting in the kitchen while she sleeps, and I rise and go to bed—too tired to keep watch, believe.

Easter at the zoo for agnostics

On Easter morning,
we took our daughter to the zoo.
We wanted to show her some of the crazy
accidents—a tomato frog, flare-nostrilled
sloth, curtain-hook claws.

My husband said sloths
stay still so long algae grows
on their fur while they sleep, though only

if the conditions are right, not here.

•

Two spider monkeys at the long window
looked out to light and trees.
One seemed depressed. The other
got up, swung rope to rope
with purpose, as if training
for military service.

She got up, once, to sniff the residual
scent of him on concrete. Then returned
to her post, chin on the back of her wrist
but not resting there.

•

Our daughter loved the smaller
squirrel monkeys best—laughed so hard
she bashed her face on the glass.

After that,
they weren't so funny but a bit
confusing—separated from us

by what?

•

On the way home,
I saw the wind yank a white
yard waste bag
from an old man's hands
as he stooped to cover
what I hadn't seen: the grey
fur of a dog, its back
to the road, not the man's
pet but a wild coyote.

That's what made me look;
I guess that's what
it gets.

•

What separates us—love or pain
or something else, lying dead on
the concrete and grass meridian?

We believe things, or see
only if the conditions
are right. Something

hard, like glass.

Learning to speak and not to speak

For more than a year now I've been quiet—
like the Spanish teacher I had one summer
who claimed to have said nothing her first year
in Mexico—until one day, sewing, she understood
everything. That's the way my daughter and I kneel
in the grass, sniffing to bestow identity on the wild clover.
My child who looks sometimes like my mother looked
dying—cheeks full of the brown fat that keeps life viable.
How close everything in the world is to its extreme
opposite. Eight hours a day the summer
mom died—*te amo, yo no puedo*

hablar. My daughter, too, waiting to speak. So far
language is what we say when she points to what
she longs for. Or maybe longing comes later, once
our tongue has found its grip, lost its grasp—
my husband waiting for me one day after class
beside the post where I had locked my bike,
hands folded in his lap. His posture, without
speaking, sufficient to the circumstance.
What slips away when pain comes?
Isn't it words that leave us first
—the right ones—whatever
likely story once made us
intelligible to ourselves.

* *te amo* = I love you
** *yo no puedo* / *hablar* = I cannot / speak

Things I can and cannot do

I cannot paint the daisies in this vase, the flagrant tangle of stem and
leaves I once mistook for dill, pinched between my thumb and finger
and, yes, tasted. Weedy as grass on the tongue of the child I was when
you taught me to brave the worn world, pack it in a red bucket, tamp
it down with my yellow shovel. You had faith in transformations, taught
me certain essential elements could ensure a miracle: stray pebbles
collected to form a moat, a dirty grey feather with a pure white quill.
The top of the bucket must be tapped to release the castle, the quill
slipped in, belief carved out. You taught me anything upended becomes
its opposite, that death is not the end of us.

At the lake, our wet, flat sand has returned to formlessness, a void. I cannot
bring you back from the dead. But I have collected the necessary materials,
built my castle on the sand. What is left holds the shape of its container,
absence. But this is not the miracle to me anymore. When something arcs
across the distance, I want to watch it go. I know that's the only way I'll
find you. Daisies grow like weeds here, and taste like what they are.

Preserve of the useful

Going back into the world after so long, lips cracked
with cold, finding the way back in through the usual portals—
snow, leaves, wind. In the backyard, hands pick crabapples
from the bare-leafed tree, fill a small box, flimsy
with frost and damp. Hands sort leaves,
and sticks, pinch the dried blooms that in spring
blew across the mind, carrying a haze
of pink air tinged with something mortal,
and sweet, lasting just a week.

At the base of each red frosted fruit, a dead flower.
The fruit is what's gathered. Whatever whole thing grows
useful out of beauty, whatever thing can last. Hands, passed down,
form the same gestures—and this is the whole purpose?
Red apples float in the yellow bowl that was once hers,
and has never not been part of the world I know.
That's trust before it's broken—objects persist
through time, the bowl is unbroken,
the tree will not be cut down.

Sonnet for the distance between us

Your garden, once ten blocks from my front door.
Red fence open, I'd find you poking dirt
with a plain fork to tend sorrel, onions.
Now this: 817 kms by plane.
I've sensed this distance before, from the air—
Rockies exposed beneath cloud like jawbones
or vertebrae, a splayed mass of the earth's
indifferent core. Where I write this poem
the ground is frozen. You go walking, snap
photos of impending spring, new buds, not
knowing inside what is bound to happen
will soon begin. Then you, speculum-scraped,

aerated, will call to say despite this
distance the fence still swings open, sorrel.

Lightening up

I say I'm trying
to practice *laughing, lightening up.*
But it feels a bit grim, like Malvolio
folding himself in the only shape he believed
Olivia would love. When he found out
it was all a joke, he hung his head. Even after
retaliation turns grave, the audience keeps laughing.
Many years ago, in the cheap theatre, I saw *Fear
and Loathing in Las Vegas*, surrounded by merriment.
As the film developed, laughter intensified—while I
shuddered with recognition. *What is the nature of
being human*, we are prone to asking? Sometimes
implication precedes understanding, but the latter
does not always follow. We are only light relative
to what surrounds us, dark by the same measure.
Shadows are always lengthening—except when
the sun is highest, at midday. Then darkness coils
beneath its object, tries to disappear.

Birth weight

I've been trying to write a poem of pure joy
to place next to the ones too full of sorrow—

It isn't like this, is it? Opposites come bound
together, the weight of an object determined

by the pull it exerts on what surrounds it. This
is why we announce pounds and ounces even

before names: we want to know what's landed
here, how far the scales have tipped, or maybe

what it cost in pain, pressure. *That's a big baby*,
they kept saying, *that's a really big baby*. 9 lbs

12 ozs, once I'd nursed him, my son's vernixy
skull soft with dark hair, my chest rivered

with sweat. Our transformational effort together
to arrive, allow arrival. The scale is birth's attendant

ontologist. What a thing weighs distinguishes it
from what it isn't: tells us what we are, are not.

Divides us so we can begin to love, continue
to grow. We say a weight and divide in two, replicate

the first miracle: the one that got us here. Coupling;
separating. We come bound to one another until someone

cuts the connection, calls it delivery, afterbirth: we
wait. Perhaps we are waiting for latch, each momentary

repair. Anyone who keeps a garden knows the first
joy of spring is perennials, the hardy green leaves—

Knows too past joy the next necessity is ruthless.
A hand a spade a quick hard yank.

Lessening

for Colin Bernhardt

In 48 hours, the feeling will begin to
lessen, he called later to reassure me.
I'd taken a paper to him, folded so
the words wouldn't show. I wanted
to find my voice, I thought that's why
I came. But he asked me to dance
around the room, instead. When he saw
me drag my feet across the floor
he had mercy. He brought me to the window
—one wall of the studio all glass—
had me shout my poem to the listening
trees. In him, practice gave facility.

After, he told me he knew grief too.
His parents dead too soon: his premonition
an altered awareness. Mine came later, as
metaphor, a hindsight. In me, what needed
to ease couldn't. He asked me to lie down.

He said: *Where in your body do you feel this?*
I said nothing, pointed to my chest, heart
burrowed in my throat, hiding where a
voice should be. He held my head in his
hands, tears on his thumbs, and spoke
my words so I could hear them. He saw
I couldn't move my grief, so he held my
head still—let grief move me.

Stories are for transforming ourselves

I.

In Deepa Mehta's *Earth*, a man is tied to two Jeeps—
for being Hindu, or Muslim, I can't remember.
I drink Scotch, I'm nineteen, I say *this is what art
is for*, to create the inner vow, the one that says
what I will never do. Years pass. I read a story
of a woman whose spine will never straighten,
whose pain won't be assuaged. When she was two,
her stepfather threw her across their living room.
I think of my mother's friend whose back ached
every day of her adult life until she stood before
her father's grave, spat in the dust (remembering
the saliva of Christ which, mixed with clay, cured
blindness) and said, teeth clenched, *I hate you* but

II.

you are forgiven. X-rays before and after that day
corroborated her miracle, what she already knew—
a corrected spine, tissue that, relieved of the effort
of tugging her body straight, could now begin to heal.
My stepfather threw his glasses across the room
let them clatter off the wall, his forehead blue
with veins, anger he had no doubt inherited.
After, he curled like a fetus on the floor, fists
balled to his chest, *I hate myself* and

III.

just like the others in this story, I have graves
to spit in, weep for, reasons to kneel before my
children, bent by what I carry. I must remember,
for them, I am larger than any story. Horror is not
the hard part to believe in; my children need me

to eat rage the way a plant absorbs the wastes
of human respiration, expires what we can breathe.
So I must change what I inherit, transform
blindness into that miracle, a cure for
blindness. The Jeeps in Deepa Mehta's film
drive away in opposite directions; here,
on earth, the parts are played by real people.

Some of what we know about airports in the 21st century

Some of what we know about winter light and the flight of birds
or waiting in long queues of astonishingly ordinary people

like us, or whom we could love, or wouldn't want to. I guess I've been
heartbroken a long time without knowing it—we do this. Go without

knowing as if the content of our propositions has anything to do
with the great fire fuelled by God-knows-what that's bruised

the horizon. Just as the flare of the refinery and all violent
condemnation makes a bruise in the heart of this terrified world.

Maybe the thing each of us doesn't want to believe in
is what fuels us, our guilt and love fluttering where the walls

meet the ceiling like those birds that live in airports disoriented
by light and warmth they can't leave, even if it doesn't nourish them.

The birds arrive as we do, through the boarding tunnels: hungry,
carrying everything we need, or believe we do, or the one thing

we were able to find. The birds are usually sparrows and enjoy
the plants and the water features, like us. It's only cold in here

because the sun's turned away. House sparrows tolerate the noise
well but suffer, in the end, from lack of darkness. Most of us have

seen them congregating up there, singing to a sky that won't be
reached by available means. Maybe we know only what we must.

Scourge of janitors, those charged with keeping up appearances, birds
can by found by attentive travellers everywhere from Edmonton to Singapore.

Inside anything, at any time: locate a container for something strange.
Geocaching in airports has reached an all-time high, despite the fact

enthusiasts are still taking more than they ever put back. Most airports
sport massive viewing windows, but hardly anyone's looking through.

Even so, the sun rises over tarmac. But if you know anything
you know this. You know it's not the sun that turns away.

Vanity

I.

The spirit *is* the animal in us.
Not two points at opposite ends
of a two-dimensional line, but a
single point, like now and Eternity.
Nor are spirit and animal opposed
to one another in any other way
(nor are you and I) for which
the human mind can muster
metaphor. What stands fused

yet opposed to both is mind—
that mirror. What allows us to see
ourselves as we are perhaps
seen by others yet not this, not
quite, not so, for we appear
in mirrors and spoons and
all lakes reversed, inverted—
not as others see us, nor yet
as we see ourselves.

II.

Let us in the future no longer
build singular vanities, but always
three mirrors that open like wings
that, together, one head at the centre,
produce those infinite multiplications
of vision that prove the limits of any
single glimpse—Or let all narcissism
become a lake into which a heaved
stone has been cast, upsetting
stillness and myth in favour of that

miraculous, abundant chaos we are
and come from and belong to.

III.
The camera that steals the spirit
accomplishes its feat by misdirection.
Something's been replaced by something
different not just in fact, but in kind.
Presence swapped for absence—*ta da!*
Here you are! As with all the darker arts,
the magic weakens or grows stronger
in relation to our commitment
to what's visible. Therefore, we need
reasoned, passionate argument!
                              But only
as a tool is needed to know if
the house is level, not to live in.
And not to know our quivering
feral spirits with—for though they
might well still see *us* through
the one-way mirror they've been
herded to the far side of, they
at present lack the magic

to return to us through it.

Conversions

God is transforming you
says the youth pastor
(in his Sufjan shirt) to his
worried, attractive companion
while on the other side of glass
a man I knew a long time ago
who'd once turned his life around
(so we marvelled) barrels past
into peril: face unshaved, aura
clouded, on his way nowhere,
huffing smoke; wounded,
limping, snuffed.

*God is transforming all of us, all
of the time*, the youth pastor insists.
He's young enough to mean it
and I look to see what he sees—
his companion slouched & pretty,
stung by love but wanting very
much to believe him.

The man I used to know has
passed us now as if we don't
even exist. I'm reminded of
the testimonies I used to hear
in the churches of my youth.
Conversion is a prematurity,
a story told before the story
ends. You stand up and declare
what you want most in this
world to be true. Squint and
you might even believe it.

But time passes. No one's
around to say *Amen*.

You don't want to die,
not even if your old life's gone.
So you light another sentence
with a shorter fuse: *God is.*

Now you've got your sentence.
You'd better hurl it. Now
you'd better run.

What I believe now about us then

for C.

The morning of your surgery I drive across the river
accepting my part in it, how fuelled I am by what we now
know, without doubt, can't last. The awful beauty of
exhaust rising in air exactly like exhaled breath, yet also
instead of breath. Today you will be healed by being gently
harmed and I can be transfused by what rises, cloud-like,
from poison, side-lit by the slowly rising winter sun. Fog
and exhaust, cloud and breath stretched thin as the soft
cotton plug my little girl pulled last night from a bottle
of vitamin C while you and I fought quietly like adults
pretending not to fight. This quiet itself a gesture to

other wounds—our arms marked, back then, by soft
violence, thin sinking of nails in each other's flesh, *pinch me*,
we said, *so I know I'm real*. My girl knows what's real:
her belief. Last night we fought while she imagined
thin white cotton into bits—which were not, but
would become these clouds, this bridge—and spread
the pieces wide as wings on the lid of her toy box.
Look! she said, last night, her bright wild voice, her
joy tinctured by viral confusion, grown up sorrow.
Sure enough, bits of fog drift now over the bridge.
Butterfly, she exhaled, and I awoke in the night

with your sore throat, a softened heart. No need to
draw blood to prove this heart: you, the broken
pieces exist, your pain was always real. Believe
me: what exhausts us most, what wastes us, can't
last. The torn cotton already, though we couldn't
see it then, was the softly torn moons, fingernails

in our flesh, was this fog that would one day rise
lit by winter sun, this bridge. Our wings
were always wide and white, clouds
fused with exhaust, fog always
sinking, being lifted.

II

Dog years

what touches the world in one place
touches it in all: the dog's weary
licking at the water bowl how
we love one another turning hard
oxytocin response or cortisol
a bowl's rim bumping a stove's wall
fourteen good years so far that's all

The opposite of the heart

The heart's not interested
in facts; when love dies,
it wants no autopsy—

only a slow rendition of its grief
played to it, again and again,
a favourite record.

The heart knows
what the heart
wants,

       a song of its own
       loss,

not the score,
but the music.

Expiration

To expire means to die; to end and not to
exhale anymore (though it also means, simply,

to exhale once: that is the word's origin, the path
by which the further meaning first entered

language, the world). All plants and all trees
whether weeping birch or trembling

aspen; all poplars; all ferns; all creeping
& climbing vines; all tender creased red &

green leaves, whether folded in birth like the ears
of our daughter as she first sipped air (inspiration),

whether clinging by fibrous stem to a source
that isn't holding on anymore in return;

whether dead or alive, in whole or in part,
these named and unnamed things

expire: once, and for all. And what they give,
freely, into the realm of unchained things

is what we need to breathe. At life's bright
and dark core: transformation occurs

not for the sake of beauty or story but because
it must. And with the energy that is invested

in us by sun and water by God we draw up with
our roots; we give off what we can't keep.

We do: we expire. We die & these green things
they give off, they rot, they absorb what we

waste and if we ask them to store it, to hold for
us what would kill us if we kept it, what

then, what do they, what does our life
ask of us? What must we find in our lungs

and guts, red-blooded creatures that we are,
to pass on, to die from, or transform?

Separated

You will now require the ministry of all
things given. You will not want to be reading this.
But trust me: you are here, no matter how
you wish it to be otherwise. Let me ask you:
Do you always speak to yourself so grimly?
Address yourself tenderly as if you were an infant
in the gale of a bad dream. You are that lost, your grief
a colic in your body as diffuse as if your lobes
had not yet formed an apparatus for distinguishing
among pains. You are that new to this world.

You are not incapable of surviving alone.
But you must become all things to yourself now:
comforter, advocate, physician, judge. Your body
might not at first appear hurt. Do not let that throw you.
Intuit the wound and treat it, to save your life.
Apply poultices to your chest and forehead,
joints and throat. Anoint yourself with oils,
musk, balms, beeswax, the compost of thorns,
bark mulch, saliva, clay. The ministries are here,
though they are not yet visible. Open yourself
as to the first stars when sky darkens—

amazed by each sudden or slow radiance
that strengthens in darkness you are learning
to know intimately, trust. Your heart must touch
impossibility, be alive to pain you start to feel
is not pain alone but a form of intelligence—
a tool; necessity; stubbornness; a kindled
beauty; a feral, wounded love. The first chance
you have, go to the top of a mountain before dawn.

Pay attention: This is your sunrise. Make this day the first day of the rest of your life. Remember: you must begin in the cold and the dark.

I-Thou

The marriage is gone, but the work
of it is not: we are sleeping together,
It and I, in my half-vacated bed, beneath
my brand new sun yellow duvet, meant to
cover me. Meant to distract from the central
untenanted fact: our room is empty now
except for me. And the work the marriage
now is, is this: to cognize how long this
emptiness had been covered by the old
duvet, how long, in short, I have been
living with you in this exact room.

For years, I have been saying *Thou* aloud
to you and every human being I love. *Thou*,
and *Thou*, to whomever I wake to, and asking
myself to wake to, to open my eyes. And all
the time believing in the theorized reciprocity.
I have been calling to myself in the darkness,
meaning you. Meaning *Thou*. Calling myself
into presence from wherever I have fallen.
But sometimes, now, I wake up grateful without
even trying to. Sometimes I am here nakedly
and unashamed in the Thou of myself
bereft and consoled as the day I was born.

We arrive holding nothing. And so, now,
I am here. Holding nothing to my chest
like a poultice knowing It and everything
besides is Thou too. Nothing is not Thou.
This whole world. Nothing is whole
that is not also shattered in pieces and
the pieces are lodged like glass in the

palm of *Thou*. Which is to say I. Which is
to name myself with a passion I have
long lacked for all my dedicated trying.

Even this green grief bursting its buds
and branches to life in me: how should I
ask for anything other than it, than Thou?
How could I call anything but call it by
your-and-my-own name, which you
chose not to remember was yours,
and which would have been enough
to cover us, our wholly nakedness?

Adultery

We adulterate ourselves first.
Dilute the sweet holy field of God
we're meant to live in, be nourished by.
Swinging the clumsy, necessary tools
—desire, reason, pain—so they
bludgeon our very ground.
We should carry each thing
lightly, near our bodies, like mothers
nursing needs, aware of bright damage
lurking on the perimeter, or bearing
nauseous seeds of grief that grow
the way all things grow. By leaching
as they feed. We will all become soil.
What troubles us is wanting to know
the meaning of each suffering thing:
each bubbling malfunction, micro-beaded
guts of sea creatures, synapses tangled in
old dendritic branches, despairing
plastics caught high in our neighbour's tree.
We love others as we love ourselves:
fearfully. And though the antidote exists,
it will be spoiled by misapplication.
Belonging is our mothers' dying bodies, not
the live pulse of baffled, married lovers.
Home is a throbbing clarity—not of need
but of squid in that dark, deep, radiant, chosen

catastrophe to which we belong, even so,
blamelessly, that sweet holy field we know
our hearts are part of when our hearts open.

Argument

We could try this out at a bar,
over pints. Which side of the table
are you on? We would each take up
a position that later that night in bed
we would alter. You say maybe God
needed to create barriers to her own
intense affection. Time and space,
flesh and blood. So the fire in her
would not burn what it loved.
Hence: interiority, free will, luck.
Each word God spoke, you

say, became original sin,
first divorce: let there be light
but also the necessary darkness.
So each stunned, exiled creature
seeks refuge in what can never be
its home. All repair is partial,
painful—though treatment is
readily available. Beauty is the
shadows of leaves, concrete, sky
broken and bruised by light,
darkness. Our desires are cries
to exiled fractured Gods of failed
omniscience who keep trying to
heal us, foolishly, by listening
to what we say.

On being in love

We live, die, in love whether or not
we experience it—as the octopus lives
and tends her doomed eggs tenderly while
slowly, herself, starving. Listen: she
is not wishing it were otherwise.
She is simply being with things as they are.
She listens to the brilliant music
her body makes by its heat and pain
and loneliness. She has grieved
the necessary presence of everything.

Fidelity

I allowed myself
to want to die
for five minutes.
I thought: *I want to*
be like Baikal. Our
old shepherd cross
who'd bled from her
nose, swiped her own
blood away with a paw.
You drove away with her
in my seat of our car.
Her ears back, eyes soft
with submission, love.
Guilt-less. Dogs are.

Our vet, your friend,
took care of it, as is said.
I wished someone for
just five minutes would
take care of me. Instead,
I heard a latch spring. You
stood open as a window
in our kitchen, making
yourself a piece of toast.

I shot like a ghost across
the air to where you were.
I saw you had always been
making this toast. You would
make it again. The piece you
had made was not for me.

I used to think love
then was proof of
love now
but it is only proof
something lived.
Certain things
put us to sleep;
others wake us.

You didn't, so I had
mercy on me: lay my
slack heart down
in the grass
for five minutes

and tried to hear
in the roots of the
grass what was true
enough to keep me
alive by knowing it,
what was left now
what was mine

to love or leave to
take care of.

Weeping birch

You stop by the house
to pick up the kids: *that birch
is completely dead on top, huh.* I nod.

I've been knowing it will happen.
Watching, from below, where the leaves
respond to breezes, substantiate storms, absorb

certain wavelengths. Trying to store up
what I love and will lose, like seeds in the
Svalbard Vault, for once it's gone. Maybe

this sounds like a lot of grief for one tree.
But for years I've been listening alone, lying
on my side in bed in the late summer light,

memorizing the wind, and force, and rustle,
the fragmented light, serrated leaves, crushed
sky, perfumed horizon, bruised quick of green,

the mortal tincture. Air charged with something
birch rendered beautiful—presence, or a keening, or
maybe just a metaphor I could not yet see.

It's called progressive dieback, what happens
once bronze borer beetles have infested the crown.
Birch trees in our city had been falling

down or being felled for years, by then.
We know this happens: lot by lot.

Theology

It is all here. The black limousine
beside the grave they will bear
your body to one day, though today
it is mere periphery. Driving home
to the home that is not only yours
but belongs to all its future tenants,
ghosts. Here are the lilacs you missed
pressing your face to the year your
mother died, and here the man
you wanted who didn't want you
enough to change everything that
happened next. Omnipresence is
no mere attribute of the divine
nature, but a fact of life. No?
We are fractured, always, by being
what we are in time and space
packing guts and hearts that
grieve and heal only by touching
our limits unboundedly, being
everywhere and all at once.

Biology

Let the pleasures return now from their exiles.
Let the long slumbers end. Let the fields fill
with rain, let wings be released from sleep.
Let the almanacs be wrong. Let drought cease
and famine pass, herds thicken and cattle graze.
Let the spirits rise from the ground with sudden
heat, dazed by their bodies, all that tugs them
closer to that current, sweeps them away: home.
Let us now dazzle the grass as it dazzles us. Let us
be one among the many souls of things, flung
awake into air dreaming still and remembering
even the long unconscious winters, the deaths
we have suffered, and will suffer, without fearing

their return. Let us buzz together with fractious
indelicate joy; let us go all the way through with it
as dragonflies do in the bright blue returning
of summer's need, heat, together again
in the chaos of belonging to everything, fully
so that anything or anyone among us by
touching or not touching might transform
us, what we are at the quick.

The fine thinking

This is not the fine thinking—
this trudging through
grass as tall as I am—
heavy boots
pinning the nettle
to the side.

The fine thinking is not this
shovel sunk in clay,
not the leverage
of the muscle,
not the hard work
of clearing the roots,
live aspen, from the ground.

The fine thinking
is not the body, nor the
mountain. Nor yet the future
we don't know
we won't share.
No—the fine thinking
is this leaf caught
in the crowns of the horsetail
by the lake—
their dried out stalks,
thin wooden flutes—

the fine thinking
is this wind
that lifts the roots
of my hair
at the scalp,

that makes the marsh grass
dance,
then bow down.

Heart

One year past
the day you left
my heart, a hurt
mammal curled
to protect its
organs, but

also, this—
instrument of
discernment, more
finely-tuned than
before, old piano
touched for

the first time
in years. Fall-
board lifted,
keys depressed
hammering all
the right notes

even though,
after this, maybe
no one will
sit down and
play again for
years—

even so.

Friendship

That summer
my mom, dying,
and me trying to
become enough
to see her through

I went to Sechelt
a line of beach along
the Sunshine Coast

my best friend's
hands cupped not
in prayer, directly,

but to teach me
how to make
a sound

call of the loon
across the ocean: it
took patience and
practice, like anything
worth experiencing

and now I know
wherever I am
how to put my
hands together
at any time

to call out
across the vast
loneliness, ask
for love
for beauty in loss
for the call

of the loon,
enough to see
me through.

Sonnet to myself and a stranger

Weep, before speaking: this is how I will
know you, not by some ridiculous rose
pinned to your lapel. Blind. Is there any
other way to find love? I am listening,
just in case. If a single sense fails, we
count on the four that don't. Is this foolish?
If I could know you by telemetry,
or other remote measure, could I solve
the mute unanswerable sorrow at
this world's dark heart? No. Proximity is
the only art. We all take comfort where
there is none to spare. Please don't speak, for I
am resolved not to answer you. If you
must: weep. Only then will love reveal us.

Incandescent light

The world says one thing, intones the
preacher. *God says another.* Heads
down, all the bright children scrawl
drawings of imaginary burrows: dark
caves where creatures can be what they
are & *world* is not a place apart. Where
children are *of* it & not only *in* it & love
is not a cave from which you stumble blind
to light and bloodied by ascent. Call it
trauma, or karma: the heart evangelized
flees, always, the scene of the lie. Exile

is unrequited love's past life: witness
the halo of pure grief. Desire needs no
remission, just permission to be what it is,
a self-healing wound. Don't get me wrong.
It hurts like hell. It takes a body down
to that dark burrow, the world, which is
of you as much as you are *of yourself* & where
you sense the very thing you, as a bright child,
knew must be there: worms, dank air, earth,
the tuber of your terrified understanding.
Yet, beneath the threshold of visible light
where things go—underground—to die

and survive there is a bountiful glow,
inefficient as love itself, produced by all
this decomposition. The spirit is a lonely
filament. It longs—as the body longs—
for heat. To burn, and *not be consumed.*
You scrawl someone's name on the wall.
You are so alive it hurts now—

struck, match-like, by what you love,
incandescent as home. You want this world
& your unrequited love & God at last
to speak the same language. Even if that
means you lie down in the dark, alone.

Elegy

Cow parsnip,
umbels of wedding lace
elegance of *Le Diner en Blanc*,
sparkle in darkness—*umbels*
voiced occasionally, each
year for eleven years as our
anniversary slipped past,
years accrued, we touched
things that touched us
or didn't, things I
squandered—your
throat, just-shaved skin,
taste of you: bitter

hops, faint pipe-smoke,
hum of sweat and good
work, blue dragonflies
in long grasses, low-
voiced song. The first
time I heard your
morning voice break
the dawn—a catch in it,
something clearing after
the night's short sleep,
our tangled limbs,

dreams—I miss most
the surprises of love
its rewarded attentions
ecologies of intimate
gifts—the funny way
you pronounce

sar-sap-a-rilla
every loved thing
I still attend to along
the edge of the path from
creased green infancy
to summer's fullness,
familiar autumnal

decompositions:
regret is homeopathic
contemplation, a search
for tender nettles in which
to roll, alone, naked. Did I
look closely enough while

what I wanted was still offered? Should I
have listened more attentively
to the language of your body
as we moved wordlessly together
in grassland, aspen parkland, boreal
forest, alpine meadows, clearings,
the world, our home?

You left in the summer that grew
out of the first spring I didn't hear
a white-throated sparrow
sing at all—I should have
understood the portents.
I asked you to stay, await
joy, but heard, instead
of my most well-loved
song, yours:

vireo
on a red-eye
flight—sunrise
mnemonic for what
had already passed
through—

And still—
Do you take this?
Yes, I do.
All the trembling
beauty too.

Ecstasis

I was a bit of a holy child
loved the verses I memorized
and worked to conform
my whole soul to—
to the good
Lord's will—of course I did.
I wanted to be on the right
side of vengeance. I knew
love: the lilt of my dad's
Northern Ireland, how it
carried his vowels off
warbling—

how his eyes
danced like candles
mischief and goodness in him
as surely as they live anywhere
on earth, and always coexist
if either one is true.

Of course I wanted to be
the child whose faith is pure
enough to call
God down
to earth
to ask for miracles: I could
have been an ecstatic, a whirling
body on the earth
translating the live wire of
God into vowels that go
warbling, consonants
that stand still and

listen—I would have been
a preacher, like my dad,
untroubled by faith, doubt.
That's how well I had
been loved by the flickering
light in him, his kind eyes,
how fully I had been nourished
by the earth, my mother's garden,
loaves of bread, miraculous

stories: when
at four years old
I began to see what else
existed: his pain and this world's
darkness, the absence of

God, how love is
powerless, and bereft—
and terminal—
and this is how I truly
came to faith: by way
of desperation: *Please,*
God, don't let him die.
I wrote songs, read verses,
revised lyrics, sang my

faithful, willed
holiness into rooms
of the house which was
neither earth nor
heaven but closer,
by then, to hell: he
no longer flickered
like a candle with

mischief and love,
but soon, by pain,
became extinguished.
He couldn't kneel

on the floor.
I couldn't climb
on his back though I wanted
strawberries, pea shoots, and for
him to shake it off, pop the clutch,
make me whirl, laugh: I wanted
to build sandcastles to the sky
at the lake we never, even
after, drove to again
because
pain is the barrier
the one we can't cross.
He no longer:

felled trees,
built fires, nor
spoke nor ate
but bled
like a saviour
though all
redemption
failed.

Still, I imagined
I might have my own
secret power. I stared
into light, clasped hands,
prayed hard: a cleft
darkening with the effort

in my heart, a splinter
driven between
mystery and

misery, though I promised
everything to God, already
faith had calved like a
doomed glacier: *Please,*
God, don't

just let him die.
And when he did die,
then, of course, I knew,
I had equivocated: I had
wanted pain to end
more than I had sought
holiness, glory. It was my
fault, the flaw in me,
a fracture along which
I would keep being displaced

until the earthquake that
punishes or goads or upends—
but always changes the ground—
arrived. So the live wire buried
in me came loose and I am
holding it still, ecstatic with
grief: I am still speaking

in tongues
translating pain
into words that go
warbling, believing
in secret power, the

yoking and splintering
of light and darkness,
which always coexist
if either one is true.
I'm living far from home,
that garden. I've lived my life

among the barriers. But also:
with stars overhead, breezes,
the clear, dark sky. So I am
starting to remember, to desire
memories—
not only death but how good
life was, and love, and
how strong which is not
the same as powerful—
or is it? Or is even
dead love, even
grief

a latent
ecstasy—the whirling
stars in darkness, light—
the shock

of living
of touching the live wire

resuscitation.

Circles

When our daughter says *stinging nettle*,
it sounds like *singing meadow*. And that's not all

she knows how to transform. She's doubled my vision.
At the optometrist's, circles drop into place at regular intervals.

Click: better *now?* Click: or *now?*—too quick, I can't tell, all
I see is the blur, the ambiguity of perception—*now?*—click—and

she runs down the moon-blown hill, globes of spent dandelions
illuminating the afternoon. Clouds flush pink then dusk-grey.

All day, I've been trying to teach her about fairness, about shapes
of objects, how circles are the same in every direction just as

the sky appears to be round like a bowl above us, its blue
at once miraculous and purely scientific—a click—and something

falls into place. *Perfect*, the optometrist says, restores my sight.
Yet it's not perfect, no vision is. Yet here she is—

ploughing through the sunlit field, mouthing the shapes
of words she hasn't learned the sting of,

singing in the meadow. Here she is loving every seed
the wind seizes—loving—yes I can see now—

—yes of course now I can see now—
equally imperfectly in all directions.

Dancing the path to understanding

Sitting in the audience tonight listening to strings
rub strings in the dark like the frenzied wings of insects
who want to mate—and, so, survive. Though you
aren't here the memory of you is flickering in me
like filaments in light bulbs at the VIA Rail station
this morning where I left you before the sun
even rose all lit up against the dark. I'm here;
the train you're on is stopped on the tracks
squandering moonlight; I'm watching Pascal
the Quebecois fiddler working with his feet
to artfully dislodge the desired feeling, dancing
the path to understanding, like a bee before bees,
while I regard, from behind, the dark heads
of the others closest to me. Heads still as
stone monuments, yet acute with compound
longing. I'm told *lens-bearing eyes*

have evolved at least seven times, so perhaps
there is still something missing, something
we do not yet see. I close my eyes
to listen, to isolate the message, that nectar
we only find if someone else waggles
revelation. That practiced disclosure, art,
is what we live on; it's what we eat, how
we love; it's what all the work sometimes
miraculously amounts to, yet doesn't
guarantee. How hard it is to break through
noise into music. The fiddle's yearning is not lonely
in the darkness but accompanied by bass
notes, the heart's acoustic strum; sadness
like ours isn't empty but filled with what
surrounds it—as a dance contains
the path it cannot name.

Breathing in the northern forest

A few degrees below zero. The after-midnight sky lit by fluorescent moons the colour of weak tea. Driving home, you saw aurora break the hasp of night over the river and slide like a hand between two buttons. There, you said, steering down the road. I caught a glimpse. This was the first time in months I'd felt that twist at the back of the neck that comes to dissolve longing: how I'd been waiting for this, what is needed revealing itself only at the precise moment it arrives. All winter, pigeons on the wire. Then one day, they make you weep. Recognizing this, not as sadness but as what in us breeds hope: aurora, a breath down a shirt when the air is too cold, when we are warmed only by what we can expel. Pull over. This is my old neighbourhood. Your hand at the back of my neck, hey, over here, and aurora, a breath beneath ribs, leaking through. The punctate lesions where the eyes fail, recognizing darkness. The colour green before it is born. Marionette strings in the dark, practicing dancing. Our chins tipped to the sky, awake-eyed, mouths held still as boreal cup-fungus. As if we could draw the light down here with our heaviness. I see you in the north glow, trace of the vanished boreal. Surrounded by absence of the forest you love. The love you taught me—white-throat, coral root. I've loved you back for five migrations through the sun. Now these lights teach volatility, the shifting of valences, the awful possibility of wanting more. A snowflake falls on your shoulder and melts, and is attached by nothing. These are the ghosts that tug at our wrists. These are the shed moments the day couldn't use, come back to tell us about weight, about how to exchange what we don't want for what wants us—particles for light. Sun-flares for the marionette strings that practice dancing. This must be how we first became spirit. This light in the north, bone-bare and drunk on wind. Breathing, even when no one is looking.

Acknowledgements

Thank you to the editors of the following publications, in which a number of the poems in this collection originally appeared: *The Fiddlehead, Grain, Literary Review of Canada, The Malahat Review, The New Quarterly.*

Thanks to Jason Lee Norman, who published "On Being in Love" as part of his YEG coffee sleeve project. #yegwords

The title of "A solstice is an astronomical event" is excerpted from https://en.wikipedia.org/wiki/solstice.

These poems were written over a ten-year period. Thank you to the friends and family members who have accompanied me through this decade with grace and good cheer. In particular, thank you to the following poets, whose generosity of spirit and editorial insight at key moments helped to shape this manuscript and to bring it more fully into being: Bert Almon, Benjamin Hertwig, Jessica Hiemstra, Erin Knight, Don McKay. I'm going to add Jack Gilbert here, too, even though we never met. *The Great Fires (Poems 1982–1992)* made me want to write a slow book: I did.

Thanks, always, to my little beauties, Juniper and Harris, for love and light, daily.

Thank you to the Edmonton Arts Council and the Alberta Foundation for the Arts for financial support during the time I wrote these poems.

Thank you, lastly, to Peter Midgley and everyone else at University of Alberta Press for bringing this little book into the world.

Other Titles from The University of Alberta Press

Demeter Goes Skydiving

SUSAN MCCASLIN

Award-winning poet exercises
the profound mother-
daughter trauma forged in the
Demeter-Persephone myth
with unapologetic modernity.

Wells

JENNA BUTLER

Through poetry, Jenna Butler
pieces together the life of
a cherished grandmother lost
to Alzheimer's.

Memory's Daughter

ALICE MAJOR

Listen to the voices of the
muses in a Scottish-Canadian
daughter's homage to
her parents.

More information at www.uap.ualberta.ca